AUDIO ACCESS INCLUDED
Recorded Piano Accompaniments Online

CELLO & PIANO

LES MISÉRABLES

FOR CLASSICAL PLAYERS

T0071346

All Songs in this edition copyright © 1980, 1986, and 1991 by
ALAIN BOUBLIL MUSIC LIMITED (ASCAP)
c/o Spielman Koenigsberg & Parker, LLP
1675 Broadway, 20th Floor, New York, New York 10019
Tel: (212) 453-2500 Fax: (212) 453-2550 e-mail: ABML@skpny.com

Unauthorized reproduction of any part of this publication by any means including photocopying is an infringement of copyrights.
International Copyright Secured All Rights Reserved

™Logo and artwork © Cameron Mackintosh Ltd.

Dramatic Performance Rights controlled and licensed by:
Cameron Mackintosh Ltd.
One Bedford Square, London WC1B 3RB England
Tel (20) 7637 8866 Fax (20) 7436 2683

Stock, Amateur and School Edition Performance Rights are licensed by
Music Theatre International, Inc.
423 West 55th Street, Second Floor, New York, NY 10019, USA
Tel (212) 541-4684 Fax (212) 397-4684
Licensing@MTIshows.com

Non-Dramatic and Concert Performance Rights are controlled by
ALAIN BOUBLIL MUSIC LIMITED (ASCAP)
c/o Spielman Koenigsberg & Parker, LLP
1675 Broadway, 20th Floor, New York, NY 10019
Tel: (212) 453-2500 Fax: (212) 453-2550 e-mail: ABML@skpny.com

'Do You Hear The People Sing' Concerts
BOUBERG PRODUCTIONS LIMITED
c/o Spielman Koenigsberg & Parker, LLP
1675 Broadway, 20th Floor, New York, NY 10019
Tel: (212) 453-2500 Fax: (212) 453-2550 e-mail: ABML@skpny.com

Unauthorized reproduction of any part of this publication by any means including
photocopying is an infringement of copyrights.
International Copyright Secured All Rights Reserved

ISBN 978-1-5400-3755-8

To access companion recorded piano accompaniments online, visit:
www.halleonard.com/mylibrary

Enter Code
3243-1574-6417-1353

HAL•LEONARD®

For all works contained herein:
Unauthorized copying, arranging, adapting, recording, Internet posting, public performance,
or other distribution of the music in this publication is an infringement of copyright.
Infringers are liable under the law.

Visit Hal Leonard Online at
www.halleonard.com

Contact us:
Hal Leonard
7777 West Bluemound Road
Milwaukee, WI 53213
Email: info@halleonard.com

In Europe, contact:
Hal Leonard Europe Limited
42 Wigmore Street
Marylebone, London, W1U 2RN
Email: info@halleonardeurope.com

In Australia, contact:
Hal Leonard Australia Pty. Ltd.
4 Lentara Court
Cheltenham, Victoria, 3192 Australia
Email: info@halleonard.com.au

HOW TO USE HAL LEONARD ONLINE AUDIO

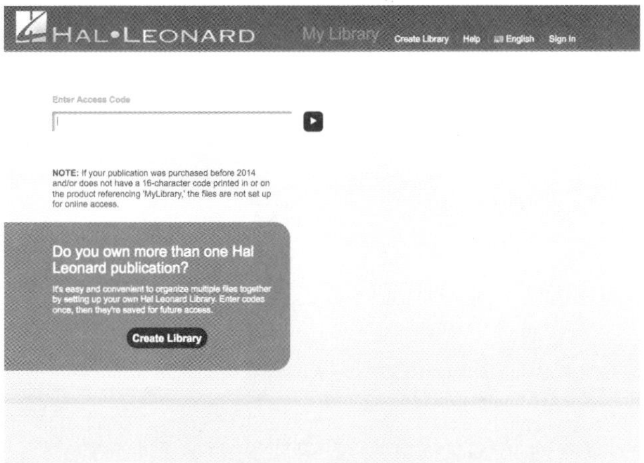

Because of the changing use of media, and the fact that fewer people are using CDs, we have made a shift to companion audio accessible online. In many cases, rather than a book with CD, we now have a book with an access code for online audio, including performances, accompaniments or diction lessons. Each copy of each book has a unique access code. We call this Hal Leonard created system "My Library." It's simple to use.

Go to www.halleonard.com/mylibrary and enter the unique access code found on page one of a relevant book/audio package.

The audio tracks can be streamed or downloaded. If you download the tracks on your computer, you can add the files to a CD or to your digital music library, and use them anywhere without being online. See below for comments about Apple and Android mobile devices.

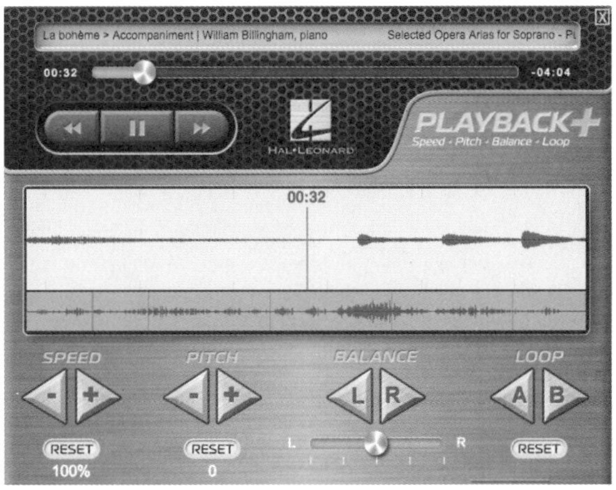

There are some great benefits to the My Library system. ***Playback+*** is exclusive to Hal Leonard, and when connected to the Internet with this multi-functional audio player you can:

- Change tempo without changing pitch
- Transpose to any key

Optionally, you can create a My Library account, and store all the companion audio you have purchased there. Access your account online at any time, from any device, by logging into your account at www.halleonard.com/mylibrary. Technical help may be found at www.halleonard.com/mylibrary/help/

Apple/iOS

Question: *On my iPad and iPhone, the Download links just open another browser tab and play the track. How come this doesn't really download?*

Answer: The Safari iOS browser will not allow you to download audio files directly in iTunes or other apps. There are several ways to work around this:

- You can download normally on your desktop computer, saving the files to iTunes. Then, you can sync your iOS device directly to your computer, or sync your iTunes content using an iCloud account.
- There are many third-party apps which allow you to download files from websites into the app's own file manager for easy retrieval and playback.

Android

Files are always downloaded to the same location, which is a folder usually called "Downloads" (this may vary slightly depending on what browser is used (Chrome, Firefox, etc)). Chrome uses a system app called "Downloads" where files can be accessed at any time. Firefox and some other browsers store downloaded files within a "Downloads" folder in the browser itself.

Recently-downloaded files can be accessed from the Notification bar; swiping down will show the downloaded files as a new "card", which you tap on to open. Opening a file depends on what apps are installed on the Android device. Audio files are opened in the device's default audio app. If a file type does not have a default app assigned to it, the Android system alerts the user.

CONTENTS

Pianists on the recordings: [1] Brendan Fox, [2] Ruben Piirainen [3] Richard Walters

The price of this publication includes access to companion recorded piano accompaniments online, for download or for streaming, using the unique code found on the title page. Visit www.halleonard.com/mylibrary and enter the access code.

At the End of the Day

Music by Claude-Michel Schönberg
Lyrics by Alain Boublil, Jean-Marc Natel
and Herbert Kretzmer

Music and French Lyrics Copyright © 1980 by Editions Musicales Alain Boublil
English Lyrics Copyright © 1986 by Alain Boublil Music Ltd. (ASCAP)
This edition Copyright © 2019 by Alain Boublil Music Ltd. (ASCAP)
Mechanical and Publication Rights for the U.S.A. Administered by Alain Boublil Music Ltd. (ASCAP)
c/o Spielman Koenigsberg & Parker, LLP, Richard Koenigsberg,
1675 Broadway, 20th Floor, New York, NY 10019, Tel 212-453-2500, Fax 212-453-2550, ABML@skpny.com
International Copyright Secured. All Rights Reserved. This music is copyright. Photocopying is illegal.
All Performance Rights Restricted.

9
mp sub.
f
12
1.
2.
14
16
mf

18
20
mf
22
mp sub.
f
mp sub.
f
25
f

27
f
29
f
31
33
mp sub.
mp sub.
f
f

Bring Him Home

Music by Claude-Michel Schönberg
Lyrics by Herbert Kretzmer and Alain Boublil

Music and English Lyrics Copyright © 1986 by Alain Boublil Music Ltd. (ASCAP)
French Lyrics Copyright © 1991 by Editions Musicales Alain Boublil
This edition Copyright © 2019 by Alain Boublil Music Ltd. (ASCAP)
Mechanical and Publication Rights for the U.S.A. Administered by Alain Boublil Music Ltd. (ASCAP)
c/o Spielman Koenigsberg & Parker LLP, Richard Koenigsberg, 1675 Broadway, 20th Floor, New York NY 10019,
Tel 212-453-2500, Fax 212-453-2550, ABML@skpny.com
International Copyright Secured. All Rights Reserved. This music is copyright. Photocopying is illegal.
All Performance Rights Restricted.

17
21
mp
rall.
rall.
25
più mosso
mf
mf
più mosso
29
rall.
a tempo
f
rall.
f a tempo

33
mp
rall.
pp
mp
rall.
pp
Tempo primo
37
mp
41
cresc.
mf
45
mf

49
53
più mosso
f
più mosso
rall.
rall.
57
a tempo
mp
p
mp a tempo
61
rall. molto
a tempo
rall.
pp
p
dim.
rall. molto
pp a tempo
dim.
rall.

Castle on a Cloud

Music by Claude-Michel Schönberg
Lyrics by Alain Boublil, Jean-Marc Natel
and Herbert Kretzmer

Music and French Lyrics Copyright © 1980 by Editions Musicales Alain Boublil
English Lyrics Copyright © 1986 by Alain Boublil Music Ltd. (ASCAP)
This edition Copyright © 2019 by Alain Boublil Music Ltd. (ASCAP)
Mechanical and Publication Rights for the U.S.A. Administered by Alain Boublil Music Ltd. (ASCAP)
c/o Spielman Koenigsberg & Parker, LLP, Richard Koenigsberg,
1675 Broadway, 20th Floor, New York, NY 10019, Tel 212-453-2500, Fax 212-453-2550, ABML@skpny.com
International Copyright Secured. All Rights Reserved. This music is copyright. Photocopying is illegal.
All Performance Rights Restricted.

7
9
1.
11
2.
mf
mf
13

15
rall.
decresc.
p
rall.
a tempo
17
19
21
rall.
rall.

Do You Hear the People Sing?

Music by Claude-Michel Schönberg
Lyrics by Alain Boublil, Jean-Marc Natel
and Herbert Kretzmer

Music and French Lyrics Copyright © 1980 by Editions Musicales Alain Boublil
English Lyrics Copyright © 1986 by Alain Boublil Music Ltd. (ASCAP)
This edition Copyright © 2019 by Alain Boublil Music Ltd. (ASCAP)
Mechanical and Publication Rights for the U.S.A. Administered by Alain Boublil Music Ltd. (ASCAP)
c/o Spielman Koenigsberg & Parker, LLP, Richard Koenigsberg,
1675 Broadway, 20th Floor, New York, NY 10019, Tel 212-453-2500, Fax 212-453-2550, ABML@skpny.com
International Copyright Secured. All Rights Reserved. This music is copyright. Photocopying is illegal.
All Performance Rights Restricted.

7
9
mf
11
mf
13

15
f
f
17
simile
19
21

23
mp
mp
25
27
29
cresc.
cresc.
f
f

31
33
35
Maestoso
37
ff

Drink with Me

(To Days Gone By)

Music by Claude-Michel Schönberg
Lyrics by Alain Boublil and Herbert Kretzmer

Music and English Lyrics Copyright © 1986 by Alain Boublil Music Ltd. (ASCAP)
French Lyrics Copyright © 1991 by Editions Musicales Alain Boublil
This edition Copyright © 2019 by Alain Boublil Music Ltd. (ASCAP)
Mechanical and Publication Rights for the U.S.A. Administered by Alain Boublil Music Ltd. (ASCAP)
c/o Spielman Koenigsberg & Parker, LLP, Richard Koenigsberg,
1675 Broadway, 20th Floor, New York, NY 10019, Tel 212-453-2500, Fax 212-453-2550, ABML@skpny.com
International Copyright Secured. All Rights Reserved. This music is copyright. Photocopying is illegal.
All Performance Rights Restricted.

14
mp
17
p
20
23

26
mf
mf
29
mp
mp
32
mf
cresc.
35
mf

38
f
41
cresc.
f
44
mp
dim.
mf
46

Empty Chairs at Empty Tables

Music by Claude-Michel Schönberg
Lyrics by Alain Boublil and Herbert Kretzmer

Music and English Lyrics Copyright © 1986 by Alain Boublil Music Ltd. (ASCAP)
French Lyrics Copyright © 1991 by Editions Musicales Alain Boublil
This edition Copyright © 2019 by Alain Boublil Music Ltd. (ASCAP)
Mechanical and Publication Rights for the U.S.A. Administered by Alain Boublil Music Ltd. (ASCAP)
c/o Spielman Koenigsberg & Parker, LLP, Richard Koenigsberg,
1675 Broadway, 20th Floor, New York, NY 10019, Tel 212-453-2500, Fax 212-453-2550, ABML@skpny.com
International Copyright Secured. All Rights Reserved. This music is copyright. Photocopying is illegal.
All Performance Rights Restricted.

13
17
Più mosso
mf
mf
21
25
f
f

29
rall.
p
rall.
33
Tempo primo
37
41
Più mosso
mf
appassionato
f

45
decresc.
decresc.
49
accel.
rall.
Più mosso
mp
f
mp
accel.
rall.
f
53
molto rall.
mp
p
dim. molto
molto rall.
p
57
rall.
Tempo primo
rall.
rall.
pp
p
rall.

A Little Fall of Rain

Music by Claude-Michel Schönberg
Lyrics by Alain Boublil, Jean-Marc Natel
and Herbert Kretzmer

Music and French Lyrics Copyright © 1980 by Editions Musicales Alain Boublil
English Lyrics Copyright © 1986 by Alain Boublil Music Ltd. (ASCAP)
This edition Copyright © 2019 by Alain Boublil Music Ltd. (ASCAP)
Mechanical and Publication Rights for the U.S.A. Administered by Alain Boublil Music Ltd. (ASCAP)
c/o Spielman Koenigsberg & Parker, LLP, Richard Koenigsberg,
1675 Broadway, 20th Floor, New York, NY 10019, Tel 212-453-2500, Fax 212-453-2550, ABML@skpny.com
International Copyright Secured. All Rights Reserved. This music is copyright. Photocopying is illegal.
All Performance Rights Restricted.

9
poco accel.
poco accel.
11
Più mosso
mf
mf
13
poco rall.
cresc.
poco rall.
a tempo
mp
mp a tempo
16
poco rall.
poco rall.

18
a tempo
p
p a tempo
20
3
22
accel.
cresc.
rall.
a tempo
p
cresc.
accel.
rall.
p a tempo
25
3

27
accel.
Più mosso
mf
accel.
mf
30
rall.
Tempo primo
pp
rall.
pp
33
mf
35
Più lento (in 8)
p
p

37
40
pp
pp
43
rall.
a tempo
ppp
rall.
pp
a tempo
3
45
rall.
rall.

I Dreamed a Dream

Music by Claude-Michel Schönberg
Lyrics by Alain Boublil, Jean-Marc Natel
and Herbert Kretzmer

Music and French Lyrics Copyright © 1980 by Editions Musicales Alain Boublil
English Lyrics Copyright © 1986 by Alain Boublil Music Ltd. (ASCAP)
This edition Copyright © 2019 by Alain Boublil Music Ltd. (ASCAP)
Mechanical and Publication Rights for the U.S.A. Administered by Alain Boublil Music Ltd. (ASCAP)
c/o Spielman Koenigsberg & Parker, LLP, Richard Koenigsberg,
1675 Broadway, 20th Floor, New York, NY 10019, Tel 212-453-2500, Fax 212-453-2550, ABML@skpny.com
International Copyright Secured. All Rights Reserved. This music is copyright. Photocopying is illegal.
All Performance Rights Restricted.

13
16
Poco più mosso
19
mf
mf
22

25
mp
cresc.
mp
cresc.
28
rit.
a tempo
f
mp
f
rit.
mp
a tempo
31
34

37
cresc.
Più mosso
39
f
3
42
45
cresc.

47
f appassionato
49
52
rit.
ff
dim. e rit.
mp
a tempo
p a tempo
55
rit.

On My Own

Music by Claude-Michel Schönberg
Lyrics by Alain Boublil, Jean-Marc Natel,
Herbert Kretzmer, John Caird
and Trevor Nunn

Music and French Lyrics Copyright © 1980 by Editions Musicales Alain Boublil
English Lyrics Copyright © 1986 by Alain Boublil Music Ltd. (ASCAP)
This edition Copyright © 2019 by Alain Boublil Music Ltd. (ASCAP)
Mechanical and Publication Rights for the U.S.A. Administered by Alain Boublil Music Ltd. (ASCAP)
c/o Spielman Koenigsberg & Parker, LLP, Richard Koenigsberg,
1675 Broadway, 20th Floor, New York, NY 10019, Tel 212-453-2500, Fax 212-453-2550, ABML@skpny.com
International Copyright Secured. All Rights Reserved. This music is copyright. Photocopying is illegal.
All Performance Rights Restricted.

9
opt. repeat
11
Più mosso
mf
mf
13
16

19
mf
21
23
25
f
molto cresc.

27
f
30
33
p
p
36
rall.
rall.

The Thénardier Waltz of Treachery

Music by Claude-Michel Schönberg
Lyrics by Alain Boublil, Jean-Marc Natel
and Herbert Kretzmer

Music and French Lyrics Copyright © 1980 by Editions Musicales Alain Boublil
English Lyrics Copyright © 1986 by Alain Boublil Music Ltd. (ASCAP)
This edition Copyright © 2019 by Alain Boublil Music Ltd. (ASCAP)
Mechanical and Publication Rights for the U.S.A. Administered by Alain Boublil Music Ltd. (ASCAP)
c/o Spielman Koenigsberg & Parker, LLP, Richard Koenigsberg,
1675 Broadway, 20th Floor, New York, NY 10019, Tel 212-453-2500, Fax 212-453-2550, ABML@skpny.com
International Copyright Secured. All Rights Reserved. This music is copyright. Photocopying is illegal.
All Performance Rights Restricted.

15
20
25
29
rall.
rall.

33
8va
f
37
(8va)
41
(8va)
mf
45
(8va)
rall.
rall.
f
f

Stars

Music by Claude-Michel Schönberg
Lyrics by Herbert Kretzmer and Alain Boublil

Music and English Lyrics Copyright © 1986 by Alain Boublil Music Ltd. (ASCAP)
French Lyrics Copyright © 1991 by Editions Musicales Alain Boublil
This edition Copyright © 2019 by Alain Boublil Music Ltd. (ASCAP)
Mechanical and Publication Rights for the U.S.A. Administered by Alain Boublil Music Ltd. (ASCAP)
c/o Spielman Koenigsberg & Parker, LLP, Richard Koenigsberg,
1675 Broadway, 20th Floor, New York, NY 10019, Tel 212-453-2500, Fax 212-453-2550, ABML@skpny.com
International Copyright Secured. All Rights Reserved. This music is copyright. Photocopying is illegal.
All Performance Rights Restricted.

10
mp
mp
12
14
mf
cresc.
16
mf
dim.
8va
7

19
p
4
8va
p
22
loco
25
27
mp
mp

29
31
mf
cresc.
mf
33
rall.
mf
a tempo
f
mp
rall.
f a tempo
36
4

38
41
dim.
44
47
rall.
rall.

Who Am I?

Music by Claude-Michel Schönberg
Lyrics by Alain Boublil, Jean-Marc Natel
and Herbert Kretzmer

Music and French Lyrics Copyright © 1980 by Editions Musicales Alain Boublil
English Lyrics Copyright © 1986 by Alain Boublil Music Ltd. (ASCAP)
This edition Copyright © 2019 by Alain Boublil Music Ltd. (ASCAP)
Mechanical and Publication Rights for the U.S.A. Administered by Alain Boublil Music Ltd. (ASCAP)
c/o Spielman Koenigsberg & Parker, LLP, Richard Koenigsberg,
1675 Broadway, 20th Floor, New York, NY 10019, Tel 212-453-2500, Fax 212-453-2550, ABML@skpny.com
International Copyright Secured. All Rights Reserved. This music is copyright. Photocopying is illegal.
All Performance Rights Restricted.

7
mp
8
p
p
10
mp
cresc.
12
mf
mf

14
16
rall.
f
8va
f rall.
17
a tempo
f
f a tempo
19

20
ff
22
rall.
8va
f rall.
24
a tempo
ff a tempo
26